RICHMOND C.

NORTH YORKSHIRE

ST AGATHA'S ABBEY, EASBY

NORTH YORKSHIRE

John Goodall, PhD FSA

❖ CONTENTS ❖

Published by English Heritage, 23 Savile Row, London W1S 2ET
www.english-heritage.org.uk

© English Heritage 2001

First published by English Heritage 2001, reprinted 2003

Photographs, unless otherwise specified, were taken by English Heritage
Photographic Unit and remain the copyright of English Heritage
(Photographic Library 020 7973 3339)

Edited by Lorimer Poultney
Design by Mercer Design
Artwork by Hardlines
Printed in England by Empress Litho

LP C50 00004 ISBN 1 85074 793 8 07/03

RICHMOND CASTLE
INTRODUCTION

Set spectacularly above the precipitous valley of the River Swale, the great castle of Richmond was the heart of one of the largest estates of medieval England. The Honour of Richmond was a vast inheritance of land extending over eight counties, and grew out of a gift made by William the Conqueror to Alan Rufus, Count of Penthièvre in Brittany. Count Alan organised these lands to maintain an ambitiously conceived castle at Richmond. The huge triangular castle site that he chose, which became known as 'the strong hill' or 'Riche Mount', was enclosed within massive stone walls and provided with a magnificent residence, Scolland's Hall. Many of Count Alan's buildings survive and form the most complete surviving example of an eleventh-century castle in the country.

The present tower keep was added and the Cockpit enclosure to the south-east of the site was fortified in stone in the mid twelfth century.

Various domestic buildings were erected, and renovations intermittently undertaken within the castle by the Crown in the thirteenth century. But its acknowledged owners in the meantime – it had passed by inheritance to the Dukes of Brittany - did not develop the castle and from the fourteenth century it fell into ruin. It remained in this condition until 1855, when a barrack block was built for the local militia. During the First World War conscientious objectors were imprisoned in cells in the castle.

Richmond Bridge and Castle: Sunrise (c.1799) by J. M. W. Turner

TOUR AND DESCRIPTION

T HIS GUIDEBOOK OFFERS a tour of the whole castle starting from the barbican courtyard, in which the ticket office stands. If you follow the instructions in italics, the tour will lead you from there into the castle enclosure and clockwise around the entire site, ending at the keep. Should you wish to follow your own route, however, the plan on page 5 will help to orientate you.

View of the castle from the east, with the Cockpit in the foreground

THE BARBICAN

You are now standing roughly in the centre of medieval Richmond, in plan a great circular fortified enclosure above the valley of the River Swale. Nearly three-quarters of this circular area is occupied by the town, but the remainder, cut out of the whole like a triangular slice of cake, is the castle. At the tip of this slice – towering

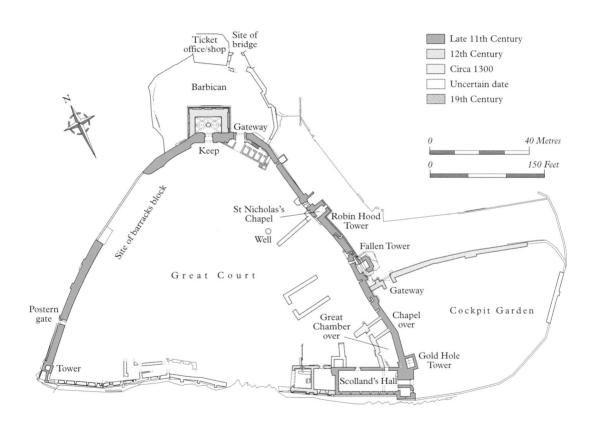

Site of bridge

Ticket office/shop

Barbican

Gateway

Keep

Late 11th Century
12th Century
Circa 1300
Uncertain date
19th Century

0   40 Metres

0   150 Feet

N

Site of barracks block

St Nicholas's Chapel

Robin Hood Tower

Well

Fallen Tower

Great Court

Gateway

Postern gate

Cockpit Garden

Great Chamber over

Chapel over

Tower

Gold Hole Tower

Scolland's Hall

immediately over you and set on the peak of the hill to dominate the town and castle alike – is the keep. The height and strength of this massive building symbolise the power of its twelfth-century builder, Duke Conan. Indeed, the facade in front of you may have been designed as an architectural backdrop for his lordly appearances before the people of the town. On the first floor, and directly overlooking the market place, are three ornamented windows, the central one distinguished from its neighbours by a 'tympanum' or semicircular stone which fills in its head.

The regular, circular plan of medieval Richmond, still preserved in the modern street layout, suggests that town and castle were laid out together in the eleventh century

SKYSCAN BALLOON PHOTOGRAPHY

Several twelfth-century keeps – such as Dover and Newcastle – had balconies set over their principal entrance on which the king probably appeared on public occasions, and these openings at Richmond could plausibly have served the same purpose for Duke Conan. The ghost of a medieval 'barbican', or outer fortification to the main castle gate, is preserved in the jumbled plan of houses and walls forming the courtyard around the keep today.

Very little of the barbican remains above ground, but it is pictured in its late medieval form in a fifteenth-century drawing (see page 18). From the combined evidence of this drawing and a survey of the buildings taken in 1538, it is clear that the barbican was a walled enclosure separated from the town by a ditch. It was fortified with three turrets and access to it was provided from the market place by a bridge with a gatehouse at its head. This gatehouse had its own portcullis and drawbridge and incorporated a porter's lodge.

The barbican was probably first laid out with wooden fortifications when the castle was established in the eleventh century and the bridge to it is first documented before 1171. The main castle gateway is a modern reconstruction of the twelfth-century entrance to the castle which stood on this site. In its medieval form it was protected by a portcullis and gatehouse tower. The eleventh-century entrance to the castle still survives but will be discussed in the description of the keep.

ROBIN HOOD TOWER

Pass through the castle gate and walk downhill along the wall to your left (east) until you reach the first tower along its length.

The main triangular enclosure of the castle is still surrounded for much of its length by an eleventh-century curtain wall, a uniquely well-preserved example of such early fortification. All the principal medieval domestic buildings were ranged against this wall. Most have now disappeared, but the various doors in the wall, the stone foundations in the lawn and the well beside you were once related to them. The great expanse of the castle interior has probably always stood open, as it does today. You are now standing in front of the so-called Robin Hood Tower, one of two towers that formerly existed along the eastern line of the enclosure.

This tower was built in two stages. As first constructed in the late eleventh century it probably only rose as high as the adjacent curtain wall walk and was crowned with battlements. It contained two barrel-vaulted chambers set one above the other and these still survive in their entirety. The use of the upper

chamber – formerly entered down a short corridor running inside the curtain wall – is not known, but the ground-floor room was a chapel dedicated to St Nicholas. This is probably the castle chapel which was given to the Abbey of St Mary in York in 1089.

Two further storeys, now largely ruined, were added to the tower in the later Middle Ages, possibly as part of Edward I's improvements to the castle in about 1300. The lower of these probably served as a bedchamber and the remains of the large fireplace which heated it are still visible in the open shell of the ruin. At the same time, a walkway was jettied out behind the tower. This allowed people to pass between the two lengths of curtain wall divided by the tower without descending to the ground. The line of stone brackets that supported this walkway are still visible.

St Nicholas's Chapel

Pass through the ground-floor doorway at the back of the tower into St Nicholas's Chapel

This chapel is a rare, if much mutilated, surviving example of an eleventh-century interior. Entering this small barrel-vaulted chamber, the visitor is faced by a cluster of windows in the east wall: a central

Items excavated from the castle:

Bone pin

Medieval glazed jugs

Lead bucket

A reconstruction drawing by Terry Ball of how the interior of St Nicholas's Chapel may have appeared

The exterior of the Robin Hood Tower. The projection around the lower window highlights the position of the chapel altar

arch flanked to either side by roundels. This triple composition formed a backdrop to the altar, the liturgical centrepiece of the interior. The altar stone was set in the deep recess of the central window, which is also provided with two niches. On the exterior of the tower, this altar window is framed by a projecting block of stonework, an architectural device to highlight the location of the chapel on the outside of the building.

A stone bench and an arched arcade run round the remaining three walls of the chapel. The arcade was formerly supported on columns, but all have been torn away. In this arrangement, quite common in castle chapel designs, each arch served as a canopy for a seat. Traces of red paint, part of a medieval decorative scheme representing masonry, are visible in the altar arch. There may have been a panel of stained glass set in the shallow recess around the damaged inner rim of the stone frame to the altar window. The seating for a rectangular shutter to close the inside of this window is also visible.

Leave the chapel and continue walking down the wall until you reach the cluster of ruins at the bottom corner of the castle enclosure.

DOMESTIC BUILDINGS

These ruins are the remains of the principal residential buildings in the castle: the great hall and inner

apartments of successive lords of Richmond. Intact within them is one of the most important surviving examples of early medieval domestic architecture in the country, Scolland's Hall. This was probably built in the 1080s but underwent extensive alteration and extension around 1300, perhaps as the result of a fire.

The ruins of the whole domestic complex of buildings are arranged today on an L-shaped plan. Along the curtain wall to your left (east), and forming one arm of the L, is a range of ruined buildings. The remaining partition walls, which divide the range into two sections, contain lines of square sockets for floor timbers. These prove that there was an upper floor to this range and also that it formerly extended northwards in a third two-storey section.

A survey of the buildings taken in 1538 describes the three upper rooms of the complete range as forming a great chamber – the principal inner apartment of a late medieval/Tudor house – a chapel and a 'chapel chamber'. This latter room probably stood in the lost north section of the range. Beside it was the chapel, clearly identified by the remains of a grand west window and piscina (washbasin) in the south wall. The remaining room must have served as the great chamber. From the fragmentary architectural details that remain this whole range would appear to have been built around 1300.

Scolland's Hall

Adjoining this range at right angles, and dominating the present cluster of ruins, is the eleventh-century hall block. Since the Middle Ages this building has been called Scolland's Hall after a constable of the castle who died between 1146 and 1150. Scolland may have been in service for upwards of sixty years and this could explain why the building was named after him. Aside from the great tower of Chepstow Castle (built 1066–71), with which it shows some affinities, this is perhaps the earliest domestic interior to survive in England.

The hall block is a two-storey structure with its principal apartments – a great hall and withdrawing chamber or solar – raised up on the

Scolland's Hall from the north. To the top left is the Gold Hole Tower and, running along the line of the wall beneath it, the ruins of the range built around 1300 with a chapel and great chamber

first floor above an undercroft. This first-floor arrangement is typical of early Norman and Anglo-Norman domestic architecture. As the fifteenth-century picture of the castle shows (see page 18), the building was originally battlemented. An imposing doorway set high in the wall at the end of the building to your right (west) gave direct access to the upper rooms. As befitted its position at the entrance to the great hall, this was grandly conceived with columns and a moulded inner arch, now largely torn away. A wide flight of stairs, also shown in the fifteenth-century picture, formerly gave access to the door, but only the ruined foundations of these now survive.

Walk into Scolland's Hall through the doorway at ground level to your right

The eleventh-century hall block is rectangular in plan and the level of its principal floor is clearly indicated by the facing lines of square sockets along the side walls above you. These sockets housed the ends of the timber beams supporting the floor. Both the upper and lower storey of the building comprise one large and one small room. On the upper floor the great hall occupied almost the entire length of the block, but divided off by a stone wall at the east end is a small withdrawing chamber or 'solar'. Beneath the solar is a gateway to the Cockpit, the outer enclosure of the castle. You are now standing in the remaining room in the block, the large undercroft which lay beneath the great hall.

This hall undercroft is lit with rectangular windows on the south side only and was probably used for storage. Some of the masonry around these windows is dark orange and pink, a sign that it has been exposed to intense heat. This is thought to be evidence of an undocumented fire which gutted the building and caused it to be remodelled around 1300.

Cut-away reconstruction drawing by Terry Ball of the Great Tower of Chepstow Castle in the eleventh century. Built a decade earlier than Scolland's Hall it also incorporated a raised hall

CADW

The hall above was clearly a magnificent room, the principal domestic interior of the castle where the household ate and slept. It was lined to either side with large windows and probably opened to a high-pitched roof. Originally each window comprised a pair of openings divided by a column with an external capital. Several on the right (south) side of the building survive intact. There is a shallow recess around each window which could have served either as the seating for a shutter or a wooden-framed panel of glass.

The windows to either side of the east end of the hall were altered around 1300, possibly in consequence of the fire at that time. This area was the most important part of the hall, the so-called dais end where the high table stood. One of the adjacent windows on the left (north) was turned into a door giving access to the newly built great chamber range, while that on your right (south) was enlarged to light the dais in the manner of an oriel. At the same time as these alterations were made, a decorative arcade of arches was added to the tops of the walls around the hall, parts of which survive.

At the opposite extreme of the great hall from the dais was the 'low' end of the room. The main entrance to the building opened into this area and in the eleventh century all the food served in the hall was probably brought from a kitchen in the castle bailey through this door. But around 1300 the great hall was adapted to suit new architectural fashions. Three new doors were punched through the west end of the building. The central one in place of an original window is still easy to see, but those to either side are now blocked. In classic medieval form these three doors opened from a kitchen, buttery and pantry directly into the hall and were probably screened off from the main body of the interior by a wooden screen. In the north corner of the west wall is a square-headed door to a spiral stair which gave access to the roof and battlements.

Walk out of Scolland's Hall through the door you entered. Turn right and walk up the stairs at the end of the hall block to the solar.

Solar

This small chamber is the solar to which Count Alan or his deputy could have retired from the hall to relax or sleep. It was entered through a door at the dais end of the hall and was heated by a fireplace. At the far end of the room was a window which has been enlarged, probably around 1300. When this alteration was made the walls of the chamber were also raised and the upper storey of the so-called Gold Hole Tower beside the solar built. The outlines of the original roof gables are still clearly visible as diagonal lines in the

The interior of Scolland's Hall, looking towards the 'low' end of the interior. The lines of sockets that once held the beams for the floor are clearly visible

A reconstruction by Terry Ball of the great hall looking towards the solar and the 'high' end of the interior

The east face of the solar to Scolland's Hall viewed from the Cockpit. The door to the the external gallery and the sockets for its timbers are clearly visible

Richmond Castle from the south-east, by Francis Place. This drawing from the 1690s gives some impression of the spectacular southern face of the castle before several of its buildings collapsed over the river cliff. Notice the line of square sockets along the exterior of Scolland's Hall at basement level. These are probably sockets for supporting a second external wooden gallery accessed from the west of the hall

masonry of the end walls of the chamber. But perhaps the most remarkable feature of this room is the doorway beside the ruined fireplace which opens into the air over the Cockpit. This seems to have been the entrance to an eleventh-century garden balcony. Details of this are clearest from outside.

THE COCKPIT

Walk down the stairs and take the first door on your left through the gateway under Scolland's Hall into the Cockpit. Turn round to face the end of the hall.

The east end of Scolland's Hall is designed as a massive gatehouse with a flanking tower. This tower was raised by a storey during the remodelling work around 1300. In contrast to the other eleventh-century doorways in the castle, the central gateway to this is without any carved decoration. Above the gate to the left (south) of the facade is the external door of the solar and, level with its

threshold, a series of square sockets. These presumably supported a wooden gallery and there is good reason to suppose that this was intended for recreation rather than defence. A royal survey made around 1280 records a garden 'pertaining to the castle'. The terms of this description suggest that this garden was the same as that which fills the Cockpit in a view of the castle nearly two centuries later (see page 18).

How long a garden had existed on this site is not known, but – integral to the town plan – it is likely to have been laid out when the castle was first established, and this gallery designed to overlook it like a balcony. A contemporary heritage garden designed by Neil Swanson now fills the area.

The perimeter of the Cockpit was fortified with a stone wall in the twelfth century and there are the remains of a contemporary gatehouse facing the town to the north of it. Walking through the surviving gateway of this the visitor can view the exterior

BRITISH MUSEUM

of the eleventh-century curtain wall, now buttressed in many places to prevent it falling away. Immediately beyond the gate are the ruins of a tower that has collapsed, a twin of the Robin Hood Tower beyond.

Go back into the castle and walk beyond the end of Scolland's Hall along the edge of the castle escarpment.

A line of buildings once ran along the southern perimeter of the castle above the river. A survey of the castle in 1538 records the function of several of these, but only the ruins of the kitchen, buttery and pantry that it describes may be identified. These probably stood in the building immediately beside Scolland's Hall, a twelfth-century structure to judge by its architectural details. In 1538 there also existed a bakehouse, brewhouse, pastryhouse and horsemill, as well as several 'old houses decayed'. The principal castle chapel, served by canons from nearby Egglestone Abbey, probably stood in this area but its precise location is not known.

Walk along the river perimeter of the castle until you face the archway and gate in the curtain wall opposite.

This raised arch in the wall is probably all that remains of a gatehouse built above the doorway through the curtain wall beneath. It may have formed part of a portcullis mechanism. Set beside the gate in the

wall is a plaque to Robert Baden-Powell, founder of the Boy Scouts. Extending northwards towards the keep from this point there stood a long, low Victorian barrack block which was demolished in 1931.

THE KEEP

Walk back up to the keep and stand in front of the arch opening into the basement.

The keep as it stands today is the product of four separate periods of building and repair. The first of these involved the construction of the grand archway into the ground floor. This was originally the main eleventh-

Interior of the first floor of the keep. The window sills have been in-filled but the inner openings were originally open to the floor and possibly served as balconies overlooking the market place

Cut-away drawing of the keep, showing the original arrangement of the roof sunk within the upper storey. In some details of design this tower compares with the twelfth-century keeps at Bamburgh and Carlisle

century entrance to the castle and was set in a stretch of the enclosure wall. To appreciate what it must have looked like it is necessary to go into the basement of the keep and look back at the former exterior face of the castle wall. Notice that the carved decoration of this door compares with that found on the main entrance to Scolland's Hall.

This great archway was then absorbed within an entirely new building, the great tower. It was probably Duke Conan in the mid-twelfth century who erected the present great tower over and in front of the old entrance. His masons used well-squared stones, as opposed to the rough rubble of the eleventh-century wall, and the junction between the old and new fabric is easy to see. Conan's tower follows in a tradition of square keeps which had been started in England by William the Conqueror's celebrated towers at Colchester and London. These

towers and their descendants are sophisticated works of architecture, intended physically to express the power and wealth of their owners. Appropriate to this purpose, the tower at Richmond dominates the centre of the town.

Externally the tower is an austere building decorated on each face with shallow buttresses and surmounted by four square turrets. As is typical of such buildings the roof is counter-sunk within the upper level of the tower to create a building with four storeys but only three floors. Access to the interior was through the door on the first floor. A modern stair leads to this today, but the 1538 survey records an earlier building on the site which served to house an entrance stair. This building was probably not fortified or stone-built because even early views of the castle show no sign of its remains.

Although Conan's tower is basically intact today, it has undergone major alteration and repair on two subsequent occasions. Edward I spent lavishly on Richmond Castle and he was probably responsible for reworking the interior of the building, inserting a vault in the basement and an internal spiral stair connecting the ground and first floor. The central pillar covering the well in the centre of the basement is also probably Edward I's work. In the nineteenth century numerous repairs were carried out to prevent the tower from collapsing.

Coarse rubble masonry was employed and wherever this replaces Conan's fine masonry visitors may be certain that they are looking at modern work.

After looking at the basement, walk up the stairs on your left to the entrance doorway.

The external door to the keep is carved with a repertoire of ornament found throughout the building. Passing through it the visitor enters a small lobby with two doors. These were probably ornamented like the outer door, but all the fine stonework has been stolen and replaced with rubble. The doorway to the right leads into the first floor of the building. This is a high chamber with a central pillar. Notice the three windows facing over the barbican. The sills of these windows have been in-filled from floor level and may originally have served as balconies (see page 6). At either end of the room are small rooms built into the thickness of the wall. These have been extensively rebuilt and their purpose is not now clear.

From the left lobby door a straight stair rises in the thickness of the wall to the second floor. At the top of the stair is a second lobby. A large window, now partly blocked, once lit this space and there are stone benches around the wall. This is presumably a visitors' waiting room for the main second-floor chamber. The chamber itself is magnificently proportioned and opens to the roof, a modern structure but one which gives a sense of the original design. This room probably served as a great hall, with a dais set beneath the pair of windows at the far end of the room. Behind the dais on the left is a door to a small withdrawing chamber. To the right of the dais is a second door giving access to the roof stair. Notice that these two doors are differently designed – that to the stair has a semi-circular overarch, but that to the withdrawing chamber has none. This piece of architectural signposting was intended to distinguish between doorways controlling access to thoroughfares and those to inner chambers. Originally all the doors of the interior were so identified.

The fabric of the upper storey of the tower perfectly illustrates the typical arrangement of a roof in a great square keep. Countersunk deep inside the tower is the modern roof with a flat top. The original roof was sprung at the same level as this but it rose to a point, as is illustrated by the pair of projecting stone blocks to either end of this space. These would have supported the timbers at the original apex of the roof. Opening onto the top of the roof to the west is a door, now blocked, which was probably used for maintenance. On the opposite (east) face is a dummy window. There are fine views from the parapets of the tower.

The great tower seen from the interior of the castle near the Robin Hood Tower

The archway of the original eleventh-century entrance to the castle is now incorporated within the base of the great tower built by Duke Conan

HISTORY

WHILE IT IS CLEAR that Richmond was among the numerous new castles erected across England in the immediate aftermath of the Norman Conquest of 1066, the exact circumstances of its foundation remain obscure. One twelfth-century poem credits William the Conqueror with building the castle in 1068–69. But rather more probable is the late medieval tradition that it was founded by Alan Rufus in around 1070. Count Alan was a nephew of the Conqueror and had commanded the Breton contingent of the Norman army at the Battle of Hastings. He allegedly established the castle to defend his northern estates from the dispossessed Anglo-Saxon nobility.

BRITISH LIBRARY, COTTON MS FAUSTINA B VII, fol. 72v

Early fifteenth-century illustration of Alan Rufus receiving the lands of Earl Edwin of Mercia from William the Conqueror in 1071. It was from this gift that the Castlery – and later the Honour – of Richmond were constituted

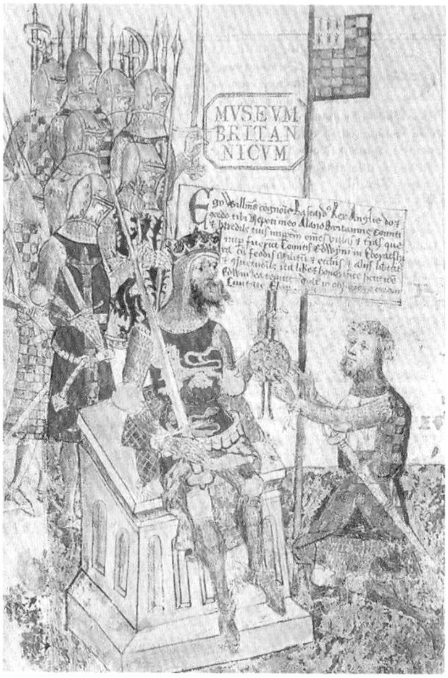

The first authoritative reference to the castle probably occurs in the Domesday survey of 1086. At this time Richmond, then called Hindrelag, was among Count Alan's possessions, one of an enormous body of estates that he owned across England. The survey entry makes no reference to a castle, but one almost certainly existed because Count Alan's lands are incidentally described as forming a 'castlery', or an estate organised to sustain a castle. That this unnamed castle stood at Richmond is implied by the fact that a core of Count Alan's lands were later constituted as an 'honour' – a

Reconstruction drawing by Terry Ball showing how the castle may have appeared in about 1400, with the addition of the keep and domestic buildings in stone

title applied to a group of properties that descended from heir to heir as a coherent estate of exceptional size – which was focused on Richmond. It seems reasonable, therefore, to interpret this Domesday allusion as proof of the castle's existence in 1086, and an early reference to what became known much later as the Honour of Richmond.

From about 1100 onwards there is a great deal of information about the medieval workings of the castlery which Count Alan established. Essentially, the lord of Richmond subleased his land to knights who agreed to perform or provide military service in return. Under this obligation of so-called 'knight service', they were obliged both to fight in the field for their lord and undertake garrison duty at Richmond Castle. Certain favoured men also received jobs in the castle – such as the posts of steward, constable and chamberlain – which gave them administrative powers in the Honour as a whole. It is apparent that many of the knights who owed service to Richmond around 1100 were Bretons.

The earliest surviving buildings at Richmond were probably erected by Count Alan in the 1080s. These include long stretches of the stone curtain wall enclosing the castle,

THE CASTLE GUARD

Preserved in the British Library is an early fifteenth-century register of documents relating to the Honour of Richmond. Among its contents are records of the so-called knight service owed by different generations of landholders within the Honour to their feudal overlord.

To illustrate this the register includes a medieval drawing of the castle viewed from the north. Displayed on banners and shields around the battlements are various coats of arms, celebrating the men responsible for different sections of the defences in the 1190s. Beneath is an extended caption which, translated freely, reads:

1. The place of Ranulph son of Robert in the castle of Richmond by the Chapel of St Nicholas

2. The place of the Constable in the enclosure of the tower (ie. the barbican)

3. The place of Brian, son of Alan, in the great hall of Scolland

4. The place of Torphini, son of Robert Manfeld, between the kitchen and brewhouse

5. The place of Ranulph, son of Henry, to the western side of Scolland's Hall

6. The place of Conan, son of Helie, beside the enclosure of the tower to the western part outside the walls

7. The place of the Chamberlain to the east of Scolland's Hall beside the oven

8. The place of Thomas de Burgo, to the west of the greater chapel of the canons within the walls.

The view does not agree in all particulars with the physical remains of the castle as it must have appeared in the late Middle Ages – quite possibly because the scribe was trying to show the buildings as he imagined that they had appeared in the 1190s - but it is obviously a likeness. Points of particular interest include the depiction of the entrance bridge, gatehouse and barbican; the greater chapel; and the garden in the Cockpit.

the great gateway embedded in the ground floor of the keep and Scolland's Hall. No other castle in England can boast so much surviving eleventh-century fabric, indeed Richmond is probably the best-preserved castle of this scale and age in the country. Having said that, it does not conform to the designs considered typical of castles in this period: it is surprisingly large and originally lacked either a great tower keep or a fortified mound, or 'motte'.

Following the death of Count Alan Rufus in 1089, Richmond Castle and its estates descended in turn to two of his younger brothers – Alan Niger and Stephen. It had passed by 1136 to his nephew, also called Alan, who was the first in his line to style himself earl of Richmond. Earl Alan married the heiress of the Duke of Brittany but died before the dukedom came into his hands. His son Conan, however, successfully asserted his claim to this title after 1156. In so doing he combined two great inheritances, that of Brittany, then effectively an independent principality, with Richmond. But Conan did not enjoy this joint inheritance for long. Unable to defend his duchy, he resigned Brittany to Henry II in 1166 and betrothed his only daughter, Constance, to the king's eldest son Geoffrey.

From the evidence of charters issued by Duke Conan it is possible to trace his movements across Europe. His visits to Richmond were a rarity, and even some of the castle officers seem to have travelled abroad with him regularly as part of his household. Nevertheless, he is credited by several medieval authorities with having built the great keep at Richmond. Such a project would have been entirely

appropriate for such a powerful man and it is probably no coincidence that he chose to place it at the corner of the castle adjacent to the market place. By this time Richmond was a prosperous town: indeed it is known to have been constituted as a borough as early as 1145.

Duke Conan died in 1171 and the castle immediately passed into royal guardianship, as is shown by Henry II's recorded expenditure on the fabric. Among the buildings listed in the Exchequer accounts as objects of repair or new work are the tower and houses of the castle (1171–74) and the 'king's house' (1186–87), presumably a reference to Scolland's Hall. Henry's son Geoffrey married Conan's heir, Constance, in 1181, but the castle may well have remained in the king's hands into the reigns of Richard I and John.

But even if the castle were held by John, the events of his reign twice put him at odds with the constable, Roald. On the first of these occasions, in 1207, Roald refused to state the value of the castle's contents for taxation. He was stripped of his office and had to buy it back with the considerable gift of 200 marks and four palfreys. The second confrontation was of a more serious nature. In 1215, the North of England revolted against John, who successfully subdued it in a rapid campaign.

The seal of Duke Conan, Duke of Brittany and Earl of Richmond. He probably built the great tower of Richmond Castle

New barrack built in 1855 to accommodate staff of the North York Militia. It was demolished in 1931

Conscientious objectors, conscripted into the army and sent to join the Non-combatant Corps at Richmond, were put in the cells as a result of their refusal to obey orders

There is no record of a siege at Richmond during the course of this, but one must have occurred because Roald is known to have been ousted from office and his garrison imprisoned in the castle by a new constable until January 1216. Forty years later, the castle is also documented as having served as a stronghold opposing Henry III after his defeat of the Montfort rebellion in 1265.

Throughout the thirteenth and fourteenth centuries the fortunes of Richmond Castle were bound up with a long-running, international dynastic dispute. Over this period it was generally acknowledged that the Honour of Richmond remained the possession of the dukes of Brittany. The price of enjoying the Honour, however, was obedience to the king of England, and this created a problem. Because of his French lands the Duke also owed fealty to the king of France. And since these two monarchs were often at war, and Brittany was rarely in a position to stand up for itself, the divided allegiance was impossible to manage. The Honour and castle were therefore periodically confiscated from the Duke and taken into the possession of either the English Crown or a royal favourite.

These changes of ownership had little direct impact on the fabric of the castle, beyond ensuring that it was not extensively altered during this period. The only recorded works were undertaken in 1250 by Henry III and by Edward I after 1294. In neither case is it clear precisely what was done to the castle, but from the evidence of the architecture it seems likely that Edward I's work was the more significant. He probably inserted the vault in the keep, renovated Scolland's Hall and extended the adjacent residential range along the east wall of the castle.

Despite these repairs, the castle gradually lapsed into ruin and a survey of 1538 shows that it was entirely derelict. It remained in this condition for the next three hundred years and became much admired as a romantic ruin. Many celebrated artists, including Turner, painted the castle and Richmond became an object of fashionable tourism. The keep was extensively repaired in the early nineteenth century to prevent its collapse.

In 1854, the Duke of Richmond leased out the castle and it became the headquarters of the North York Militia. A barrack block was erected against the west curtain wall the following year, the keep adapted as a depot and a storage block built beside the main castle gate. In 1908 the castle was designated the headquarters of the Northern Territorial Army and Robert Baden-Powell, the founder of the Scouts, briefly commanded here until 1910. That same year the army handed over the historic fabric of the

❖ CONSCIENTIOUS OBJECTORS ❖

Early in 1916, during the First World War, conscription was introduced in response to the desperate need for soldiers. Men were allowed to appeal against military service on conscientious grounds, but unless they received total exemption from locally constituted tribunals they were obliged to enter the Non-Combatant Corps. This was a uniformed branch of the army, whose men were subject to military discipline. But some of those forced into the NCC refused to be involved in any army activity at all, including drill, wearing a uniform and work touching the war effort. They were punished for their disobedience and at Richmond a number were imprisoned in a surviving group of cells created out of a storage range beside the gate. The walls of these tiny rooms are still covered in graffiti, which includes devotional quotations, diagrammatic representations of the composition of heaven, family portraits and exhortations to strength in adversity.

Eager to make an example of such conscientious objectors, the military authorities determined to send them to France. There, it would appear, they intended to charge them with disobedience to orders in the face of the enemy, for which the sentence was execution by firing squad. The so-called Richmond

Pencil drawing in one of the detention cells by John Brocklesbury, a Quaker schoolteacher from near Doncaster, who was one of the 'Richmond Sixteen'

Sixteen were illegally spirited away from the castle on 29 May 1916 and sent to a camp near Boulogne, where they were put before a tribunal on this trumped-up charge.

In the meantime desperate attempts were being made by their friends in England to find out where they were. A doctored field postcard, sent by one of the men, provided the necessary information and the circumstance became an embarrassment to the army. Consequently, in a dramatic courtroom scene, they were sentenced to death and then – after a short pause – informed that this would be commuted to ten years' hard labour. For the remainder of the war the men were dispersed around various prisons in England to serve their gaol term. Afterwards they were released, but the return to civilian life was not easy and many were socially ostracised.

castle to the Ministry of Works, but did not relinquish control of the buildings. During the First World War, the castle was occupied by the Northern Non-Combatant Corps.

The Richmond barrack block was demolished in 1931 and the castle passed from the control of the Ministry of Works to English Heritage in 1984, in whose hands it now remains.

ST AGATHA'S OR EASBY ABBEY

ST AGATHA'S MONASTERY, now known as Easby Abbey, stands about a mile downstream from Richmond Castle on the banks of the River Swale. Beside the abbey ruins is a fine parish church, and beyond this the abbey gatehouse, both worth visiting. Rather than offer a detailed tour of the site, the following section introduces the abbey complex and then describes the most important buildings within it individually.

Easby Abbey *by William Callow (1812–1908)*

TOUR AND DESCRIPTION

There are three principal elements to the ruins of the Premonstratensian Abbey of St Agatha at Easby, founded in 1152. Clustered around the cloister to the south of the site are the conventual buildings. These were the living quarters of the community and include the ruined remains of the refectory, chapter house and dormitory. To the north of the site there probably stood the infirmary, abbot's house and various ancillary buildings, such as workshops and storage rooms. Dividing these two elements of the abbey was the church, the focus of the community's daily life of prayer.

This entire monastic complex was surrounded in the Middle Ages by a high wall. Access to this walled enclosure was through the gatehouse to the south-east of the site. Just within the enclosure, beside the gatehouse, is the parish church of Easby, which was served in the

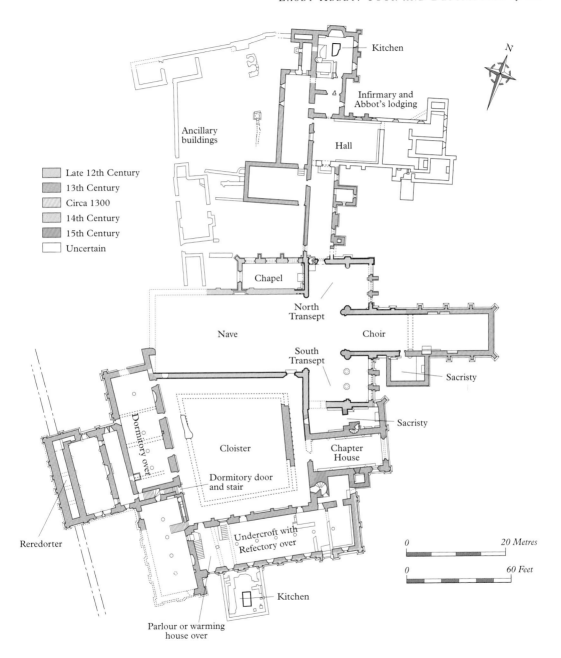

Kitchen

Infirmary and
Abbot's lodging

Ancillary
buildings

Hall

Late 12th Century
13th Century
Circa 1300
14th Century
15th Century
Uncertain

Chapel

North
Transept

Nave

Choir

South
Transept

Sacristy

Sacristy

Dormitory over

Cloister

Chapter
House

Dormitory door
and stair

Reredorter

Undercroft with
Refectory over

Kitchen

Parlour or warming
house over

0   20 Metres

0   60 Feet

The east range of the cloister with the chapter house in the centre and the sacristy to the left

Reconstruction drawing by Terry Ball of how the abbey may have appeared in about 1500

Middle Ages by a canon of the abbey. This contains some fine, but heavily restored thirteenth-century wall-paintings, and a remarkable twelfth-century panel of glass depicting St John.

With the exception of parts of the abbey church, nothing of the original twelfth-century abbey buildings survives. The plan of the monastery as it presently exists was created during the thirteenth century. The gatehouse and parts of the abbot's house were built in this period, as were most of the conventual buildings, which were erected in a complex sequence of building campaigns that progressed clockwise around the cloister. Around

1300 the refectory was remodelled in the most extravagant fashion. Some of the conventual buildings, as well as the abbot's house, were then extensively re-ordered in the late-fifteenth century. Such remodelling is characteristic of many monastic houses in this period. It is usually interpreted as evidence of the relaxed observance of the monastic life, but this does not appear to have been the case at Easby.

The Cloister and Chapter House Range

After the church, the cloister and the range of buildings along its eastern side were the first parts of the present plan to be laid out. These were erected in the early thirteenth century but were then extensively remodelled, probably between 1478 and 1482. As it was originally planned the ground floor of the range comprised three rooms, a central, vaulted chapter house – where the canons gathered formally every day with their abbot and might discuss business – flanked to either side by smaller chambers. The northern chamber between the chapter house and the church probably served as a sacristy or chapel, but the function of that to the south is not clear. A stair in the cloister beside it probably gave access to the original canons' dormitory, which in contemporary monastic plans was typically situated on the upper floor of this range. The ghost of what must be the

dormitory's high roof gable is still visible in the refectory wall.

In the fifteenth century the range was thoroughly refashioned. The upper storey was rebuilt and new windows inserted throughout. Spiral stairs to the new upper rooms were erected within the chambers to either side of the chapter house. The function of the new upper rooms is not known. On the exterior of the range there survive remains of the late medieval whitened render finish to the buildings.

THE REFECTORY

The most impressive ruin to survive at Easby is the monastic 'refectory', or dining hall, which lies to the south of the cloister. This building was originally divided into two floors: the arches along the lower walls mark the line of a stone vault and down the centre of the building are a series of stumps belonging to the pillars that supported it. This lower floor was an undercroft, probably used for storage, and was divided up internally with walls, the foundations of which run irregularly across the interior lawn.

Above this, its floor supported on the undercroft vault, was the refectory. This upper room where the canons ate their meals was a splendid work of architecture, lit along one side by high windows, each filled with a lattice of stone tracery. A fourteenth-century law case records that these windows were glazed and

decorated with coats-of-arms. At the 'high end' of the refectory, beneath the great east window, was the abbot's table. The second refectory window beneath this housed a pulpit from which a canon would have read during meals.

It was typical in monastic refectories to arrange the tables down the sides of the room with benches set behind them against the wall. This allowed servants to move around easily in the centre of the room and to serve the meals over the tables. Because of the large windows to the south, it is possible that at Easby there were only tables on one side of the room. The food itself was prepared in the kitchen which is now entirely ruinous. This stood against the south wall of the refectory at the point where the sequence of large windows is broken by a blank wall. Set in this wall is the hatch through which the food was passed.

Looking across the cloister towards the north wall of the refectory

Interior of the refectory looking towards the great east window

The refectory pulpit was set in this deep window frame. Raised above floor level it was reached up a short stair in the thickness of the wall

The thirteenth-century door to the dormitory stair includes a reworked Romanesque arch, possibly from the first buildings on the site. Beside it are the decorated arches of the lavabo, a set of basins for the canons to wash their hands in before meals

The outline of the kitchen roof gable is still visible in the exterior masonry.

Roughly facing the kitchen hatch on the ground floor of the opposite (north) wall is the main entrance to the building from the cloister. An internal stair would have risen from this to the refectory level. The line of this stair cut off one section of the building – the west bay – from the remainder. On the upper floor this area was probably partitioned off from the refectory to form a parlour, where the monks could relax at certain times of the day. At the undercroft level a stair descends to a second parlour, possibly for guests, built against the outer western end of the refectory. The importance of this stair is indicated by the fact that the corbels supporting the vault over it are carved with figures, an enrichment lacking elsewhere in the undercroft.

In its present condition the refectory is an entirely thirteenth-century structure, but it was erected in two stages. The north wall, blank except for two high windows, was probably built in the middle of the century. To judge from what remains, its interior must have been very dark, and within a generation the canons decided to correct this fault. They did this by tearing down the south side and east end of the building, virtually to foundation level, and re-erecting them with the huge windows you see today. Even the undercroft windows on the south side were enlarged, but this created a problem which has left its mark. The new windows were too high to fit under the old undercroft vault. This had to be raised up accordingly and consequently all the vault arcade arches on this side are stilted.

THE WEST RANGE

The west range was a three-storey building constructed against the rising hill of the river valley so that its middle floor opened at ground level to the cloister. It formerly extended beyond the line of the refectory to the south, but this end of the building has collapsed. Projecting behind the main range is another three-storey building with an ornamented facade overlooking the modern entrance to the abbey. Beyond this, above a channel of running water fed from the river, is the monastic latrine or 'reredorter'. The two lower storeys of these buildings were vaulted throughout. The architectural details suggest that these ruins were built in the mid-thirteenth century as part of a long-running but coherent building campaign, along with the original refectory.

The position of the reredorter shows that the monastic dormitory, usually placed nearby for convenience, occupied some part of this complex of buildings. Presumably, therefore, the original dormitory in the upper floor of the chapter house range to

the east of the cloister was abandoned when this new building was finished. The new dormitory was on the lost upper floor of the range and entered up a stair rising from the large, ornamented door facing onto the cloister. The function of the other chambers in the range is educated guesswork. Possibly the calefactory – a heated common room – was located somewhere here and the vaulted room immediately adjoining the refectory may have been a guest chamber. Some areas in the basement were probably used for storage.

THE CHURCH

Very little remains of the church today beyond the lines of its foundations. The body of the building appears to be twelfth-century, but the choir to the east was later extended and remodelled, shortly before 1300. At the same time the transept chapels were given new windows. In the late fourteenth century a new chapel was constructed against the north side of the nave.

Numerous tomb slabs are preserved in the floor of the church and in the north wall of the extended

The facade of a richly decorated building in the west range, with the reredorter block to the left

Tomb niches which may have held tombs of the Scrope family, patrons of the abbey

Access to the abbey was through the gatehouse, which had two gates controlled by a porter, one for pedestrians and one for horses and wagons

have confidently ascribed uses to them. What the surviving plan does suggest, however, is that the complex included a hall with a kitchen beyond it. The hall might have been an infirmary building, for tending the sick, which was then later adapted to form the abbot's house. Such a transformation occurred in many local monasteries, such as Rievaulx.

The buildings, which have been much altered over time, are impossible to date with any certainty. A tiny oratory on the upper floor immediately beyond the hall to the north possesses late thirteenth-century architectural detailing. There is fragmentary evidence that the buildings were radically remodelled in the fifteenth century, at the same time as work was underway to the east cloister range. The chimney that rises prominently from the ruins is probably of this date. In the lawn beside the buildings are the remains of ovens and channels, signs of lost service buildings.

The Gatehouse

The gatehouse was the main entrance to the monastic enclosure and also served as the place from which alms were distributed in the Middle Ages. It is a two-storey building of the late thirteenth century. A high passageway passes through the length of the lower storey. This is divided by a wall with two doors, one for pedestrians and one for carts. The outer part of the passage beyond the

section of the chancel are two tomb niches. These may well have housed two Scrope family tombs described by an abbot in the fourteenth century as lying in the choir of the church.

There is an unusual quantity of medieval paint surviving in the church, but it is hard to spot. The south transept preserves traces of a masonry pattern in red and white as well as colouring in the window mouldings. One of the Scrope tomb niches also includes the remains of a masonry pattern.

The Infirmary and Abbot's Lodging

Beyond the north transept of the church extend the foundations of a two-storey corridor leading to a complex of ruined buildings. We do not know what function these various structures served, though antiquarians gates served as a porch. There was an external stair to the upper floor, but the use of this room is not known. The window in the outer gable of the gatehouse is richly carved. In plan the building compares closely with the excavated remains of the gatehouse to another local Premonstratensian house, Egglestone Abbey.

❖ THE PREMONSTRATENSIANS ❖

Easby was a house of Premonstratensian canons, that is to say a group of priests living a communal religious life according to the governing statutes of the abbey of Prémontré, near Laon in France. This mother house had been founded by St Norbert in 1121 and the rule it observed had been influenced by the contemporary development of Cistercian monasticism. It sought to combine a strict communal religious life with ministering to the laity, in particular preaching and serving parishes. The order enjoyed considerable popularity in England, where about thirty Premonstratensian houses were founded during the twelfth century.

The Premonstratensians were popularly known as 'White Canons', because of the colour of the habit they wore. Confusingly, however, the

Drawing by Peter Urmston of two Premonstratensian canons, the one on the left dressed as a canon of Easby in the fifteenth century

canons of Easby were not entirely dressed in white. As a mark of favour, Pope Boniface IX (1389–1404) gave the community special licence to wear linen rochets and black birettas with their other white garments.

The Premonstratensians were unique among English religious orders (save only the Carthusians) for never having established themselves at the universities of Oxford or Cambridge. Perhaps as a result, they produced only a single bishop throughout the entire Middle Ages. But Richard Redman, who died as Bishop of Ely in 1505, regularly visited the abbeys of his order and tried to correct the problems he found. From the work he did we have an insight into the state of the whole English Premonstratensian Province on the eve of the Reformation. Of the twenty-nine houses visited during the forty-six years of Redman's work, ten were regularly and invariably praised for the state of their affairs, seven, including Easby, passed through difficulties, and the others suffered frequent problems of discipline.

HISTORY

Detail of thirteenth-century window in the three-storey block to the west of the cloister

ACCORDING TO LATE MEDIEVAL authorities, the Abbey of St Agatha at Easby was founded by Roald, Constable of Richmond Castle, in 1152. In fact, the early history of Easby was probably more complicated than this bald attribution suggests. The charter by which Roald endowed the abbey implies that a religious community already existed here. This reading of the document is borne out by the survival of fragments from an eighth-century stone cross in the parish church at Easby. These facts combined may suggest that Easby was an Anglo-Saxon 'minster', or church with a community of priests who were responsible for serving the surrounding parishes. In the twelfth century such small independent communities were under great pressure to assume the rule of a regular religious order. What probably happened at Easby under Roald's patronage, therefore, was that a centuries-old minster community

adopted the Premonstratensian rule.

Easby was the third Premonstratensian house to be established in England and was a wealthy foundation by the standards of the order. Little is known about the early history of the abbey. Modest new domestic buildings were probably erected while the abbey church was being built in the twelfth century. Then, over the course of the thirteenth century, these first generation domestic buildings were replaced on a grand scale as funds came to hand.

The refectory and parts of the abbot's lodging were then remodelled again later in the same century, possibly after extra bequests of land in 1285. After these changes there was a lull in building work to the abbey. This may in part reflect the hardships caused by the wars with Scotland.

At some date in the early fourteenth century the patronage of the abbey passed to the Scrope family, who used it as a burial church. Some surviving Scrope wills demonstrate the generosity of the family towards the abbey. Their gifts to it included vestments, liturgical instruments in precious metal and payments of cash to every canon in the community. A celebrated law suit between Sir Richard Scrope, sometime Chancellor of England and the builder of Bolton Castle in Wensleydale, and Sir Robert Grosvenor, over the use of a coat-of-arms in the 1385–90 furnishes us with some details of the abbey interior, such as the location of tombs and their decoration. In 1392–93 Sir Richard also procured a licence to donate land worth £150 per annum to the abbey. In return for this the community was to support ten additional canons, two chaplains and twenty-two poor men in perpetuity.

Between 1500 and the Reformation little is known about the community or its condition. There are conflicting assertions made about the year in which the abbey was

suppressed, but it probably surrendered to the Crown in 1536. Shortly before this, in 1534–35, it was valued at about £111 per annum. This valuation lists the numerous charitable and administrative obligations of the community, including the support of chaplains in eight Yorkshire parishes and numerous doles to the poor. The most important of these was the annual distribution of £4 worth of wheat, rye and white and red herrings on St Agatha's feast day. Like many areas of the North of England, the local populace of Richmond was deeply disaffected by the suppression of the monasteries. Stirred by this and other complaints, they joined in the Pilgrimage of Grace in 1536, the most serious popular rebellion of Henry VIII's reign. Many religious houses were briefly restored by the rebels, and Easby was among them. Henry VIII was determined to avenge this rising and, after persuading the rebels to disperse, he set about

The early sixteenth-century carved screen in Wensley Church, transferred from the abbey by the Scrope family at the Dissolution, reminds us of the rich furnishings that the abbey once contained. A set of choir stalls from the abbey can also be seen in St Mary's Church, Richmond

View from the east across the abbey ruins

❖ # VISITATIONS ❖

The most fully documented years in the history of the abbey are 1478–1500. Over this period the Principal of the English Premonstratensian Province, Richard Redman, regularly came to Easby on visitation. A visitation was a formal enquiry into the state of a community, and its findings were recorded.

In 1482, for example, Redman found that a certain John Nym was a fugitive from the community and was to be judged by a tribunal for his faults. Nym was accused of incontinence with a widow, Elizabeth Wales, but was subsequently proven innocent of the charge and by 1494 rose to be prior of the abbey. Redman directs that the abbot allow access to the calefactory before and after meals when the weather was cold; that the prior make sure that the brethren did not make dissolute conversation; that no one go to bed without a tunic, hose and girdle on pain of a day's bread and water; and that silence be properly observed. He goes on to say that the community was in debt and concludes by praising the overall state of the monastery, which was well provided with food and new buildings. This reference to new buildings may date the extensive fifteenth-century alterations to the abbey.

In other years Redman also comments about the practice of devotion in the church, educating the novices, the treatment of the sick, absence from the monastic enclosure and drinking after Compline, the last Office of the evening. Beside these statements there have also survived lists of the community over this period. These show that it fluctuated in size over the last quarter of the fifteenth century, supporting between fifteen and twenty-four brethren, including priests, deacons and novices.

exacting punishment. Writing to the Duke of Norfolk, the commander of his forces in the north, on 22 February 1537 Henry instructed: '... you must cause such dreadful execution upon a good number of the inhabitants, hanging them on trees, quartering them and setting their heads and quarters in every town, as shall be a fearful warning... [And] at your repair to Salley, Hexham, Newminster, Lanercost, St Agatha and such other places as have made resistance ... you shall without pity or circumstance cause the monks to be tied up without further delay.'

The particular fate of the canons of Easby is not known, but the lands of the abbey were subsequently leased out and the buildings allowed to fall into ruin. To judge from the earliest paintings of the site, Easby has changed little since the late seventeenth century. The ruins came into the possession of the Department of the Environment before 1936, and passed to English Heritage in 1984.